Michel Streich

GENERAL WASTE

A Scholastic Press book from Scholastic Australia

For Lisa

Scholastic Press
An imprint of Scholastic Australia Pty Limited (ABN 11 000 614 577)
PO Box 579 Gosford NSW 2250
www.scholastic.com.au

Part of the Scholastic Group
Sydney • Auckland • New York • Toronto • London • Mexico City
New Delhi • Hong Kong • Buenos Aires • Puerto Rico

Published by Scholastic Australia in 2024.

A catalogue record for this book is available from the National Library of Australia

ISBN: 978-1-76120-569-9

Typeset in New Century Schoolbook and Mind the Gap.
Design by Michel Streich and Hannah Janzen.

Michel Streich created these illustrations using digital and traditional tools.

Printed in China by Ink Asia.

Scholastic Australia's policy, in association with Ink Asia, is to use papers that are renewable and made efficiently from wood grown in responsibly managed forests, so as to minimise its environmental footprint.

10 9 8 7 6 5 4 3 2 1 24 25 26 27 28 / 2

General Waste loved stuff.
Lots and lots of stuff.

He had a different toothbrush for every day of the week,

six hairdryers . . .

and countless lotions and potions.

His house was filled with a myriad of machines, power tools, widgets and contraptions. There were so many, he could hardly remember what they were used for.

In one room, General Waste kept countless electric gadgets. He adored it when they blinked and buzzed and beeped and rattled.

*My newest one! It's **beautiful**.*

In another room, he had hundreds of fancy lamps. He always left them on, so he could see all his stuff gleaming in the bright lights.

Every day, General Waste took a ***very*** long shower, just for fun. He called it the 'hour of shower'.

And every night, General Waste
dreamt of having even more stuff.

General Waste lived on the top floor of the house.

On the bottom floor lived Gram-Gram.

Gram-Gram saved every morsel of food, and she carefully stored leftovers in her fridge. She had a pantry the size of a shed, filled with preserved vegetables, meats and fruits. Some of the food even came from her own garden.

With all this food, I'm never in a pickle . . .

General Waste threw away his food after one bite.

The first bite always tastes ***best!***

He liked his food and drink in handy little plastic containers. That way, he didn't have to clean any dishes!

Gram-Gram went everywhere on her bicycle.

General Waste enjoyed zooming around in his fourteen-wheel drive.

*Nature looks **fantastic** at high speed!*

Gram-Gram rarely bought anything new, and always dressed in clothes that were soft and comfortable from wearing and washing.

Every week, General Waste bought himself a haul of crisp new clothes.

I have to keep up with uniform fashion!

General Waste grew bored with his new things quickly. So he always had to go shopping for even newer stuff.

More and more ***and more*** stuff piled up in his house. There was the new stuff, and the old stuff, and the broken stuff, and the half-eaten stuff. There was the packaging of the stuff and the wrapping around the packaging of the stuff.

So much stuff,

that one day . . .

HELP!

Luckily, help was not far away.

Enough *with this stuff!*

Gram-Gram grabbed some old boxes and together they began sorting through the mountain of stuff.

General Waste discovered he already had everything he needed . . . and plenty to give to others.

Next, Gram-Gram showed him how to repair broken stuff, and how to make new things out of old ones.

In their breaks, they cooked together. General Waste noticed that making your own food takes time and care.

They made art together

. . . and music too.

Gram-Gram showed General Waste how to care for little things . . .

. . . and how to plant trees and vegetables, and flowers for the birds and insects. Gram-Gram used General Waste's half-eaten old snacks to make food for plants.

They even found a good use
for the fourteen-wheel drive.

One warm afternoon, General Waste and Gram-Gram were sitting in the garden with the birds and insects. He adored it when they trilled and warbled and buzzed and hummed.

At that moment, they both had the same thought . . .

***Life's too wonderful
to waste on stuff!***